IN TIME OF NEED:
PARISHES AND CANON 517, §2

Therese Guerin Sullivan, SP
Gary D. Yanus

Canon Law Society of America

ISBN: 1-932208-06-2
SAN: 237-6296

The Canon Law Society of America's programs and publications are designed solely to help canonists maintain their professional competence. In dealing with specific canonical matters, the canonist using Canon Law Society of America publications or orally conveyed information should also research original sources of authority.

Canon Law Society of America
Office of the Executive Coordinator
108 North Payne Street, Suite C
Alexandria, VA 22314-2906

TABLE OF CONTENTS

PREFACE

In a time of need as well as in a time of abundance, the Holy Spirit continues to create ever new and always holy the Church of Jesus Christ. While experiencing a scarcity of vocations to the ordained priesthood, the Church has been blessed with an abundance of lay persons seeking to serve the Body of Christ. The 1983 *Code of Canon Law* recognizes that there exist parish situations in which the ministry of a permanent pastor may not be possible. Canon 517, §2 provides for the pastoral care of a parish to be overseen by a deacon or a lay person due to a shortage of priests.

It is well known that there are many demands made on the ministry of a priest. Today priests are expected to be leaders who welcome and encourage all the baptized to participate in the mission of the Church. They are to collaborate with and encourage the role of deacons; they are to call on and celebrate the gifts of religious women and men; they are to welcome the development of lay ministries. This text, in my opinion, will be of great assistance to all in leadership in responding appropriately to these new challenges. It reflects an excellent review of the meaning and intent of Canon 517, §2 and twenty years of experience of practice in the field by two highly respected canonists serving the Diocese of Cleveland.

Most Reverend Anthony M. Pilla
Bishop of Cleveland

The text of *In Time of Need: Parishes and Canon 517, §2* is derived from a seminar presented by the authors at the 2004 Canon Law Society Convention in Pittsburgh, Pennsylvania. The authors revisit a topic first discussed in *Pastoral Care in Parishes Without a Pastor: Applications of Canon 517, §2* published in 1995 by Barbara Anne Cusack and Therese Guerin Sullivan, S.P. This older publication grew out of a 1992 study of canon 517, §2 by the Canon Law Society of America's committee on lay ministry research. *In Time of Need: Parishes and Canon 517, §2* continues the Society's mandate to CLSA Publications to promote greater understanding and application of canon law.

In Time of Need: Parishes and Canon 517, §2 addresses the situation in which, due to a shortage of priests, the diocesan bishop finds it necessary to entrust a share of the sacramental pastoral care of a parish to someone else who has not received the status of priest, or to a community of persons not included in canon 519. The new text builds upon the experience of at least one North American diocese in an attempt to implement the Inter-dicasteral Instruction, *"On certain questions regarding the collaboration of the non-ordained faithful in the sacred ministry of priest,"* 15 August 1997 in *AAS* 89 [1997] 852-877.

The text is organized into two parts. Part One delineates the job descriptions of the presbyteral moderator (priest supervisor) and the parish life coordinator (parish director) as provided for in the Diocese of Cleveland. Qualifications of the presbyteral moderator are given and the responsibilities are stated. A particular emphasis of the text is that of sacramental needs. The role of the priest supervisor in the sacramental ministry of the parish is to preside at Eucharistic celebrations; to celebrate other sacraments according to a schedule mutually arranged between him and the parish life coordinator; to afford the laity their rightful place in the celebration of the liturgy. The role description states the priest will be invited to attend, as his schedule permits, parish social events and meetings in order to establish and support pastoral contacts among the people with whom he celebrates sacraments. The responsibilities given to the parish life coordinator have been divided among four principal areas: the ministry of worship, the ministry of education, the ministry of pastoral services and the ministry of administration. The teaching of the Church regarding the role of the priest in parish life is given the emphasis of recent instructions of the Holy See. Canon 517, §2 is analyzed.

Part Two examines the role of the parish life coordinator. Full pastoral care in a parish is distinguished from the collaboration or participation in the exercise of pastoral care entrusted to a deacon or some other person who is not a priest or to a community of persons when the condition of a dearth of priests exists. The *2002 Roman Instruction: The Priest, Pastor and Leader of the Parish Community* states the preference for the assigning of a deacon in a parish without a resident pastor. Faculties granted at ordination and those authorizations that may be given to a deacon and granted to a lay person are delineated. The areas included are ministry of word, the catechumenate and Baptism, Eucharist, Marriage, other acts of divine worship and selected faculties in danger of death. Sacramental preparation is treated in the sections on Infant Baptism, Confirmation, First Penance and First Communion and Marriage. The Liturgy of the Hours is presented as a means of communal prayer.

Sample documents are included in the appendices. They include application form for the position of parish life coordinator; contract for lay employment agreement; contract for parish life coordinator; appointment letter from the bishop; mandate letter from the priest supervisor; and celebration of installation.

A selected bibliography is included.

Part I: The Parish

REVEREND GARY D. YANUS, J.C.D.

I. AN EXPERIENCE OF SACRAMENTAL MINISTRY IN A PARISH WITHOUT A RESIDENT PASTOR

A. Introduction: Saint Procop Parish, Cleveland, Ohio

On a Saturday evening in January, 2004 the temperature hovered close to 10° F. Members of the congregation of Saint Procop Church on Cleveland's Near West Side were beginning to arrive. They entered a church in which the temperature on the thermometer on the thermostat registered 36° F. Late the previous night a tunnel which runs from the Great Depression era boiler house which shelters the Korean War vintage boiler had collapsed, cutting off all heat. Upon closer examination the following Monday, it was discovered that the boiler house itself was in danger of collapse, posing not just a threat to the comfort of parishioners but because of the questionable state of the natural gas lines running in and out of the building, a potential disaster for the entire neighborhood.

More recently, a series of violent thunderstorms blew off a significant portion of the roof of the one hundred and one year old church. The state of the roof was examined, and the decision to replace it was made. A committee was formed, estimates were taken, and provisions for finding the necessary funds to pay for a new roof were made. Work began within a few weeks.

The parish possesses a convent that once housed more than twenty religious women. The convent has not had any sisters in residence for more than thirty years. After the convent was vacated by the members of the religious congregation, various diocesan and neighborhood programs have used the ample space of the old building, but the last four years the convent has been vacant and

1

falling into disrepair. A proactive approach was taken to find an appropriate use for a basically sound building. Contacts were made. Individuals came to inspect the facility. Eventually an ecumenical group expressed interest in the building which they desired to transform into a facility for transitional housing for men. Contacts were made with various city officials. The necessary permits were obtained. Meetings with the neighbors were arranged and held. Work goes forward, and many in the parish are involved in the project.

Friday evenings throughout the year a free hot meal is prepared and served in the hall of the school. Two suburban parishes assist on the second and third Fridays of the month. Because of the age and health of a number of individuals from Saint Procop Parish who prepare and serve the meal, a need developed to find assistance for one of the Friday meals each month. Contacts were made, and a city parish committed to preparing and serving the meal on the fourth Friday of each month.

After a period of several years with very few weddings, this past June six were celebrated in the parish church. Diocesan guidelines for preparing couples for marriage were followed. The couples received instructions. The Cleveland Diocesan Evaluation for Marriage was administered and discussed. The marriage liturgies were planed with care. The wedding rehearsals were conducted. Sacred celebrations were the result of pastoral instruction and sensible planning.

A priest supervisor, *presbyteral moderator*, and a parish director, *parish life coordinator*, have been assigned by the diocesan bishop to direct the ministry of Saint Procop Parish. The involvement of the priest supervisor with these few but typical scenarios of life and ministry of Saint Procop Church was primarily supportive and cooperative. The parish director, a Sister of Notre Dame, took charge of each administrative and pastoral challenge. She and the lay people of Saint Procop proposed solutions and came up with initiatives. The parish is an urban island of Christian charity and worship thanks to the creative pastoral arrangement permitted by the Bishop of Cleveland.

The letter of appointment of the *presbyteral moderator* stated that he was to be endowed "with the powers and faculties of a pastor." He was to provide supervision of the pastoral care given by the parish life coordinator of Saint Procop Parish and "assist her in those areas which require priestly ordination."

The job description as assembled by the diocese states:

> The presbyteral moderator is appointed by the bishop of the diocese to provide supervision of the pastoral care given by the parish life coordinator. He is given the rights and responsibilities of a pastor for canonical purposes. He is accountable to the bishop and collaborates with the parish life coordinator. Where the priest also serves as the sacramental minister, he is to ensure that sacramental and pastoral care, which require ordination to the priesthood, are provided to a parish entrusted to a parish life coordinator.

The qualifications of the presbyteral moderator are:

> • A deep understanding of the nature of collaborative ministry, a good communicator, and an openness to working with and accepting the role of a parish life coordinator;

> • An understanding of the baptismal call of every Christian to share in ministry to the degree possible given the current discipline of the church; and

> • An ecclesiology deeply rooted in Vatican II theology and liturgical reform. An awareness of the authorized rituals for the celebration of the sacraments.

The responsibilities have been delineated as:

> • To supervise the pastoral care of the parish and in that capacity to seek to be informed of the parish life, needs, growth, and development;

3

• To assist the parish life coordinator in the regular evaluation of the effectiveness of parish ministry;

• To ensure observance of all canonical/diocesan policies;

• To be available to the parish life coordinator for information, advice, clarification, mutual support as needed;

• To accept, assist and support the role of the parish life coordinator among the staff and parishioners;

• To preside at Eucharistic celebrations on Sunday and Holy Days of Obligation according to the schedule mutually arranged by him and the parish life coordinator; and

• To celebrate the sacraments according to a schedule mutually arranged between him and the parish life coordinator.[1]

As his schedule permits, the presbyteral moderator is to participate in meetings at which the planning takes place for liturgies at which he will preside. The priest will be invited to attend, as his schedule permits parish social events and meetings in order to establish and support pastoral contacts among the people with whom he celebrates sacraments.

• To meet regularly with the parish life coordinator to mutually assess and plan the entire scope of pastoral care provided;

• To afford the laity their rightful place in the celebration of the liturgy; and

[1] At the time of his appointment, the priest is granted general delegation to assist at all marriages within the territory of the parish.

• To serve the parish life coordinator as spiritual advisor in the affairs of the parish.

The responsibilities given to the parish director, *parish life coordinator*, have been divided among four principal areas: the ministry of worship, the ministry of education, the ministry of pastoral services, and the ministry of administration.

Within the ministry of worship the parish life coordinator is:

• To preside at daily liturgy (morning prayer, liturgy of the word and communion service) subject to the *Code of Canon Law* and the norms of the local Church;

• To preach when pastorally and canonically appropriate;

• To participate in the spiritual life and worship commission of the parish, providing spiritual and liturgical vision;

• To share in planning/evaluating of Sunday liturgies/homilies, children's and other special group or home liturgies, seasonal liturgies, Lenten mission/renewal;

• To recruit/train/organize/schedule liturgical ministers;

• To share in planning of communal penance services;

• To participate in planning and coordination of Rite of Anointing during Mass;

• To work with couples planning weddings;

• To provide guidance and direction to families arranging funerals; and

• To share in planning and coordination of the Rite of Christian Initiation of Adults.

Within the ministry of education, the parish life coordinator is:

• To participate with the Pastoral Council, providing spiritual and educational vision;

• To coordinate/direct sacramental catechesis: pre-baptismal instruction of parents, First Communion, First Penance, and Confirmation preparation, marriage preparation;

• To share in development and implementation of evangelization program;

• To direct or assist with all stages of catechumenate process;

• To organize or to facilitate adult Bible studies, prayer groups, discussions;

• To be a resource with the director of religious education for religious education programs; and

• To supervise and develop a parish book rack.

Within the ministry of pastoral services, the parish life coordinator is:

• To participate with the Pastoral Council in responding to social concerns;

• To coordinate pastoral care of the sick and elderly, enable parishioners' involvement in ministry to shut-ins and those in hospitals and nursing homes;

• To provide pastoral counseling or refer people to appropriate counseling services;

• To facilitate/coordinate parish involvement in existing community projects, i.,e., the parish life coordinator provides a liaison between parish and community agencies in meeting needs of the poor;

• To organize parish projects and on-going programs to respond to local needs;

• To be aware of available social services and make referrals as needed;

• To assist with tribunal marriage cases; and

• To serve as spiritual advisor for parish committees and groups;

Within the ministry of administration, the parish life coordinator is:

• To participate in all juridic affairs of the parish in accordance with canon law;

• To administer parish properties and income in accordance with the law;

• To participate responsibly in the business management of the parish;

• To participate actively in the establishment of policy and procedure regarding property control, equipment, and supplies in accordance with the guidelines of the Diocesan Finance Office;

• To evaluate programs periodically;

• To accept responsibility for general parish office activities;

• To utilize a planning process with the Pastoral Council and Finance Council and others to ensure effective functioning of parish programs;

• To maintain parish books of income and expenses;

• To prepare annual reports requested by the diocese;

• To prepare an annual budget of income and expenses in accordance with particular law; and

• To register and meet with new parishioners.

The challenge of a sacramental ministry is connected necessarily to comprehending the individual and unique pastoral landscape of the parish and how priestly ministry fits into that landscape. The sacramental mission of a priest supervisor differs little from that of a resident pastor. Assessing the sacramental needs of the people of a "certain community of the Christian faithful stably constituted in a particular church"[2] requires familiarity with the identity of the community itself.

Saint Procop is a non-territorial parish erected for the care of Bohemian Roman Catholics in the late nineteenth century. The flight to the suburbs which began in earnest in the period following World War II reached its apex in the late 1960s. The parish, which once operated both a grade school and a high school, included 2, 410 registered parishioners in 1960. In 2003 the *Status Animarum* reported to the Diocese of Cleveland listed a total of 361 individuals registered at Saint Procop Parish. In 1960 there were 74 baptisms, 56 first communions, 27 marriages and 58 deaths. In 2003 there were eight baptisms, one first communion, two marriages and seven deaths.

The sacramental ministry of the parish is identified by the immediate needs of those who are elderly and homebound. The regular celebration of the Eucharist, the anointing of the sick and the sacrament of reconciliation are understood as the center of the parish's sacramental ministry. Although a priest is not present in the parish twenty-four hours a day, seven days a week, the sacramental needs of the people are being met while the other forms of ministry

---

[2] Canon 515, §1, *Code of Canon Law, Latin-English Edition* (Washington: Canon Law Society of American, 1998) 168-169. Hereafter *Code of Canon Law.*

8

important to the community as a whole thrive under the direction of the parish life coordinator.

B. Role of the Priest Supervisor (Presbyteral Moderator) in the Sacramental Ministry of the Parish

The diocesan job description of the presbyteral moderator includes four specific references to the sacramental ministry of the presbyteral moderator: "1) To preside at Eucharistic celebrations; 2) To celebrate other sacraments according to a schedule mutually arranged between him and the parish life coordinator; 3) To afford the laity their rightful place in the celebration fo the liturgy; and 4) The priest will be invited to attend, as his schedule permits, parish social events and meetings in order to establish and support pastoral contacts among the people with whom he celebrates sacraments." The last provision may appear to be related only remotely to the sacramental ministry of the priest. Those who have "supplied Mass help" on weekends perhaps realize more keenly than others that effective sacramental ministry builds on relationships. The celebration of Eucharist in all contexts, Sundays, weddings, funerals, anniversaries, etc. is enhanced by pastoral familiarity. The sacraments of reconciliation and anointing are also more meaningful and more closely attached to the Paschal Mystery when celebrated by someone whose proclamation of the Word has been heard and whose preaching content has been adjusted to the specific community. The presence of the presbyteral moderator at social functions fosters a friendly dialogue that assists in the full celebration of the sacraments.

The presbyteral moderator is appointed "endowed with the powers and faculties of a pastor."[3] The "powers and faculties" of a pastor must be understood with some discretion and with appreciation for a unique pastoral situation not accepted as normative in the current legislation. The sacramental ministry of the presbyteral moderator in a pastoral arrangement foreseen by canon 517, §2 and as directed by diocesan guidelines is an essential collaborative

---

[3] Bishop Anthony M. Pilla, Letter of Appointment, protocol number, 221a/2002, April 16, 2002.

complement to the ministry of the parish life coordinator. The job description of the sacramental minister uses the term "mutually arranged" when referring to the celebration of the sacraments. With due respect given to canonical requirements regarding the celebration of the sacraments, the presbyteral moderator is also asked to work in close cooperation with the parish life coordinator in scheduling and planning the specific celebrations. The arranging of weddings, funerals, baptisms, the sacrament of reconciliation, communal penance services, and the sacrament of confirmation is to be a joint effort. The process of bringing adults into the Church through the celebration of the *Rite of Christian Initiation of Adults* is to be also a collaborative effort.

II. THE TEACHING OF THE CHURCH REGARDING THE ROLE OF THE PRIEST IN PARISH LIFE

Pope John Paul II in an allocution to the Plenary Assembly of the Congregation for the Clergy, stated:

> The function of guiding the community as shepherd, the proper function of the parish priest, stems from his unique relation to Christ the Head and Shepherd. It is a function having a sacramental character. It is not entrusted to the priest by the community, but, through the Bishop, it comes from the Lord. To reaffirm this clearly and exercise this function with humble authority is an indispensable service to truth and to ecclesial communion. The collaboration of others, who have not received this sacramental configuration to Christ, is hoped for and often necessary.

> However, these cannot in any way substitute the task of the pastor proper to the parish priest. The extreme cases of shortage of priests, that advise a more intense and extended collaboration of the faithful not honored with priestly ministry, in the pastoral care of a parish, do not constitute an exception to this essential criterion for the care of souls, as is indisputably established by the canonical norms (cf. *Code of Canon law*, c. 517, §2)...

In fulfilling his duty as guide, which is his personal responsibility, the pastor will surely obtain help from the consultative bodies foreseen by canon law (cf. *Code of Canon Law*, cc. 536-537); but these must remain faithful to their reality as consultative bodies. Therefore it will be necessary to guard oneself from any form that tends *de facto* to weaken the leadership of the parish priest, because the very structure of the parish community would be distorted. . .[4]

The Church's magisterium is not reticent to protect the sacred and unique nature of priestly ministry. There is no substitute for the parochial ministry of a priest as noted in the instruction of the Congregation for the Clergy, *The Priest, Pastor and Leader of the Parish Community*. The full care of souls "absolutely requires" the exercise of priestly orders.[5] The essential obligations of the pastor are outlined in canon 528: 1) he is obliged to see that the word of God is preached in its entirety, through the preaching of the homily and through catechetical instruction; 2) he is to foster social justice; 3) he is to promote Catholic education; 4) he is to strive to bring the Gospel message to those outside the Church; 5) he is to make the Eucharist the center of parish life; 6) he is to nourish the faith of his people through the celebration of the sacraments, especially the Most Holy Eucharist and the sacrament of penance; and 7) he is to encourage the practice of prayer in the family, active participation in the liturgy of the Church which he must supervise under the authority of the diocesan bishop.

The ministerial expectations of the parish priest are enumerated in canon 529 of the 1983 *Code of Canon Law*. The parish priest must make great effort to know the people entrusted to his care. He must visit families, seek out the poor, the afflicted, the lonely. The following duties are entrusted to the pastor in canon 530: 1) the administration of baptism; 2) the administration of the sacrament of

---

[4] Address of John Paul II to the Plenary Session of the Congregation for the Clergy, November 23, 2001 #5, *AAS* 94 (2002) 216-217.

[5] See Instruction of the Congregation of the Clergy, *The Priest, Pastor and Leader of the Parish Community,* August 4, 2002. Part II, #20, *L'Osservatore Romano*, English Edition, January 14, 2003.

confirmation to those in danger of death; 3) the administration of Viaticum and the anointing of the sick; 4) the assistance at marriages; 5) the celebration of funerals; 6) the blessing of the baptismal font during the Easter season, the leading of processions, and the imparting of solemn blessings outside the church; and 7) the more solemn celebration of the Eucharist on Sundays and holy days of obligation.

It is clear that the thrust of the current canonical legislation and Roman documents is to protect the sacred and unique nature of priestly ministry. In those cases in which a collaboration with the ordained ministry has been entrusted to the non-ordained faithful, "a priest must necessarily be appointed as moderator and invested with the power and duties of a parish priest, personally to direct pastoral care."[6]

There is opposition to permit the use of titles for a lay person in a parochial ministerial setting which include in some way the words, "pastor," "director," "coordinator," "moderator," and the like. In an instruction of the Congregation for the Clergy, *Ecclesia de mysterio, On Certain Questions Regarding the Collaboration of the Non-Ordained Faithful in the Sacred Ministry of Priest,* approved in *forma specifica* by the Holy Father and promulgated on August 15, 1997, is found the following admonition regarding the collaboration of lay persons in the pastoral ministry closely associated with that of parish priest:

> The right understanding of canon 517, §2 . . . requires that this exceptional provision be used only with strict adherence to conditions contained in it. These are:
>
> a. *ob sacerdotum penuriam* and not for reasons of convenience or ambiguous "advancement of the laity," etc.
>
> b. This is *participatio in exercitio curae pastoralis* and not directing, coordinating, moderating or governing the

---

[6] Ibid.

parish; these competencies, according to the canon, are the competencies of a priest alone.

The instruction adds,

> Because these are exceptional cases, before employing them, other possibilities should be availed of, such as using the services of retired priests still capable of such service, or entrusting several parishes to one priest or to a *coetus sacerdotum* (c. 517, §1).[7]

The solution to a shortage of ordained priests in certain parts of the world is envisioned in Roman documents not by the sharing of ministry proper to the priesthood but rather in "programs which give priority to the promotion of vocations to the Sacrament of Holy Orders."[8] In a discourse regarding the participation of the lay faithful in priestly ministry, the Holy Father concluded,

> In some local situations, generous, intelligent, solutions (to the priest shortage) have been sought. The legislation of the *Code of Canon Law* has itself provided new possibilities, which however, must be applied correctly, so as not to fall into the ambiguity of considering as ordinary and normal, solutions that were meant for extraordinary situations in which priests were lacking or in short supply.[9]

---

[7] Congregation for Clergy, Pontifical Council for the Laity, Congregation for the Doctrine of the Faith, Congregation for Divine Worship and the Discipline of the Sacraments, Congregation for Bishops, Congregation for the Evangelization of Peoples, Congregation for the Institutes of Consecrated Life and the Societies of Apostolic Life, Pontifical Council for the Interpretation of Legal Texts, *Ecclesiae de mysterio, On Certain Questions Regarding the Collaboration of the Non-Ordained Faithful in the Sacred Ministry of Priests*, Practical Provisions. Article 4, §1, August 15, 1997 *AAS* 89 (1997) 866.

[8] See John Paul II, Discourse at the Symposium on "The Participation of the Lay Faithful in the Priestly Ministry" April 22, 1994, *L'Osservatore Romano*, English edition May 11, 1994.

[9] Ibid.

III. THE SOLUTION OF CANON 517, §2

Canon 517 is an innovation found in the current canonical legislation.[10] The provisions of paragraph two of canon 517 permits the entrusting of pastoral care of a parish to a deacon, a non-ordained person, or a community of presumably non-ordained persons when, due to a "scarcity" of priests, a pastor cannot be appointed. The discussion during the revision process of the code regarding this particular innovation did not enjoy unanimous enthusiasm regarding the proposal.[11] The support of the secretary of the code commission, Archbishop Rosalio José Castillo Lara, led to the eventual acceptance of the proposed law.

Archbishop Castillo Lara had been an enthusiastic supporter in his native Venezuela of religious women who had been given the care of Christian communities in rural areas. The only source of the second paragraph of canon 517 is listed as an instruction of November 19, 1976 of Propaganda Fidei, *La fonction évangelélitrice* which speaks of the role of religious women in mission territories.

Similar to the vision of the document of Propaganda Fidei, the vision of the *coetus* was that the provisions found in canon 517, §2 were to be extraordinary and temporary. The pastoral care of the parish is to be entrusted to a deacon, lay person, or group of lay persons under the supervision of a priest only because there is no pastor available due to a shortage of priests. Although the position is an ecclesiastical office,[12] no official title is given to it. The absence of an official title appears to emphasize the temporary and transitional nature of the provision for pastoral care. If and when the situation within the particular church changes and vocations are readily available to fill all diocesan offices, the parish is to be given a pastor and the arrangement under canon 517, §2 is to cease.

---

[10] See John P. Beal and others, ed., *New Commentary on the Code of Canon Law* (New York/Mahwah: Paulist Press, 2000) 682-688.

[11] See *Communicationes* 13 (1981) 147.

[12] Canon 145: §1. An ecclesiastical office is any function constituted in a stable manner by divine or ecclesiastical ordinance to be exercised for a spiritual purpose. §2. The obligations and rights proper to individual ecclesiastical offices are defined either in the law by which the office is constituted or in the decree of the competent authority by which the office is at the same time constituted and conferred." *Code of Canon Law*, 43

A "shortage," "lack," "dearth," of priests[13] is open to interpretation by the diocesan bishop. What a shortage of priests may mean to the Bishop of Cheyenne, Wyoming may mean something entirely different to the Bishop of Cleveland, Ohio. It would be reasonable also to assess the wisdom of naming a pastor to a small parish with limited needs in the context of the needs of the entire diocese. In the case of Saint Procop, the ministry of a full-time pastor entrusted with the care of less than two hundred active members is difficult to justify when there are within the same diocese parishes of over twelve hundred families with one parish priest.

The authority of the priest supervisor is not vague or inexact in the context of canon 517, §2. The canon specifies that in his role of *curam pastoralem moderetur* he is equipped with the power and faculties of a pastor although canonically the office of pastor is vacant. Faculties *ipso iure* which universal or particular legislation grants to a pastor would also be granted to a priest who is appointed by the bishop to supervise or moderate the pastoral care of a parish under the direction of a parish director.[14] Faculties to celebrate the sacrament of penance, to preach, to preside at the celebration of the sacrament of matrimony, the power to delegate other priests or deacons to preside at marriage are provided by the law itself. Additional faculties granted by the diocesan bishop would also be granted the priest supervisor.[15]

As stated above, the priest supervisor is not the pastor of the parish. But because he possesses the powers and faculties of a pastor, he may wish to "mandate" the lay minister or the deacon certain areas of responsibility. The mandates, not faculties, come from the priest supervisor and not the bishop because they are proper to him.[16] John Huels states in his recent book, *Empowerment*

---

[13] *Si ob sacerdotum penuriam* (c. 517, §2).

[14] Barbara Anne Cusack and Therese Guerin Sullivan, SP, *Pastoral Care in Parishes without a Pastor: Applications of Canon 517, §2* (Washington: Canon Law Society of America, 1995) 22.

[15] Ibid, 24. See also Appendix C, "Sample List of Faculties for Priest Supervisor," Cusack and Sullivan, 28-30.

[16] John M. Huels, J.C.D., *Empowerment for Ministry: A Complete Manual on Diocesan Faculties for Priests, Deacons, and Lay Ministers.* (New York/Mahawah: Paulist Press, 2003) 171.

for Ministry: A Complete Manual on Diocesan Faculties for Priests, Deacons, and Lay Ministers, that if the priest supervisor is not to assume the duties of administering the parish, he would be well advised to grant three mandates to the deacon or lay pastoral minister.

The deacon or pastoral minister should be mandated to act in the name of the priest supervisor to provide legal representation of the parish in accord with civil and ecclesiastical laws within the bounds of the minister's job description.[17] [18] The lay minister or deacon should also be mandated to preside at the meetings of the parish pastoral council and finance council which canon 536, §1[19] and canon 537[20] specifically allocate to the competence of the pastor.[21]

The third mandate counseled by Huels is more inclusive. A sample of this mandate states,

> You may make decisions necessary for the fulfillment of the duties enumerated in your job description and for implementing an approved pastoral plan and project. The more important decisions, as determined by the priest supervisor, and all decisions adversely affecting the rights of persons, require the prior consent of the priest supervisor; but if he cannot be reached, you may decided the matter, which decision must be confirmed by him or the local ordinary.[22]

---

[17] Canon 532: "In all juridic affairs the pastor represents the parish according to the norm of law. He is to take care that the goods of the parish are administered according to the norm of cann. 1281-1288." *Code of Canon Law*, 175

[18] Huels, *Empowerment for Ministry*, 172.

[19] Canon 536, §1: "If the diocesan bishop judges it opportune after he has heard the presbyteral council, a pastoral council is to be established in each parish, over which the pastor presides and in which the Christian faithful, together with those who share in pastoral care by virtue of their office in the parish, assist in fostering pastoral activity." *Code of Canon Law*, 177.

[20] Canon 537: "In each parish there is to be a finance council which is governed, in addition to universal law, by norms issued by the diocesan bishop and in which the Christian faithful, selected according to these same norms, are to assist the pastor in the administration of the goods of the parish, without prejudice to the prescript of can. 532. *Code of Canon Law*, 178.

[21] Huels, *Empowerment for Ministry*, 173.

[22] Huels, *Empowerment for Ministry*, 173.

Huels believes that this particular mandate permits the pastoral minister to make the mundane decisions which arrive at a pastor's door as well as those more serious decision affecting the rights of the faithful. The priest as a "supervisor" thus maintains the right to overturn a decision of the lay minister if he was not first consulted. The day to day decisions may not need to be brought before the priest supervisor. Issues involving the right to the sacraments,[23] the right to have a Christian burial with the rites of the Church,[24] and functioning as a godparent[25] or a sponsor for confirmation[26] are of such importance that the involvement of the priest supervisor can be a both a safeguard and a means of pastoral support.

IV. CONCLUSION

Pope Paul VI called the parish the center in which one lives the Christian faith. The parish is the normative and primary place in which the care of souls happens.[27] The vision of the parish as a community of faithful, he believed, implies surpassing the vision of the parish as a juridic structure for the care of souls. The parish exists for the care of souls, but it is also something more. The parish is the presence of the universal Church in a particular environment. It is of its nature missionary.

Ecclesiae imago describes the elements which make the parish the presence of the Church in large cities:

> The parish must be a community of faith, of worship, and of charity, a sign of the presence of God in the world. It must offer a certain continuity in the preaching of the Word of God and in the exercise of worship. It must constitute in every quarter of the city the personified

---

[23] See cc. 843, §1; 851, 2°; 868, §1, 2°; 913, §1; 914; 915; and 1125.
[24] See cc. 1183, §§2, 3; and 1184.
[25] See c. 874, §1, 3°.
[26] See c. 893, §1.
[27] Paul VI, Discourse to the XVI Week of Pastoral Renewal, September 9, 1966. *Insegnamenti di Paolo VI*, (Romae: Tipografia Poliglotta Vaticana,1966) 391.

presence of the Universal Church and the Diocesan Church, the presence in which Christ is ministering to the needs of the sick, the poor, the immigrants, and all the smallest brothers and sisters. The parish must assist the christianization of human relationships. It must represent the visible point of unity and universalism for the small Christian communities existing within its territory.[28]

The *Code of Canon Law* of 1983 does not ignore the pastoral problems occasioned by diminishing vocations to the ordained priesthood. It also does not ignore the great shifts in population which have occurred in the last thirty years. Into these movements within the life of the Church, the code attempts to integrate the vocations of lay persons. Canon 517 is located in the code among the canons on the parish. But the canon does not refer to a different type of parish as much as it refers to a different way to provide for pastoral care.[29]

The pastoral care of a parish, the traditional *munera* of teaching, sanctifying, and governing, is intimately connected to the exercise of priestly orders.[30] The parish priest supervisor is a collaborator in the mission of the parish who directs the scope, content, and style of pastoral care. His essential sacramental ministry nourishes and sustains the parish while uniting it to the diocesan bishop and to the universal Church. But priests are called to fulfill their responsibilities in an ecclesial spirit, as part of the community of the local church and "in collaboration with all the pastoral agents, avoiding acting in an independent, autonomous way, and fitting in with the pace of the community in achieving its goals, with patience and flexibility."[31]

Immediate needs may not be the best catalyst of legislation. The

---

[28] *Ecclesiae imago*, 175.

[29] Francisco Ramos, OP, *Le Diocesi nel Codice di Diritto Canonico.* (Romae: Millennium Romae, 1997) 448.

[30] Canon 521, §1: "To become a pastor validly, one must be in the sacred order of the presbyterate." *Code of Canon Law*, 171.

[31] Congregation for the Evangelization of Peoples, *Pastoral Guide: For Diocesan Priests in Churches Dependent on the Congregation for the Evangelization of Peoples,* October 1, 1989 in *Enchriiddion Vaticanum* vol. 11, 1580 ff.

Holy See has expressed its concerns regarding the implementation of canon 517, §2. The law allows for the means to meet the needs of the faithful in a responsible and ecclesially authentic manner which diminishes neither the image nor the ministry of the parish priest. Collaboration between the priest supervisor and parish director permits the Church to exist in sectors of the community in which there is an urgent need for the presence of the people of God. The priest is such situations is in a position to encourage convergence of action in justice, foster a spirit of unity, promote identity as a Catholic, all the while positioning himself to be an agent of transformation through the power of the sacramental life of the Church.

Part: II: The Role of the Parish Administrator

SISTER THERESE GUERIN SULLIVAN, SP, J.C.L.

I. PASTORAL CARE

A. Full Pastoral Care

Full pastoral care[32] is reserved to the priest in any parish including one where a pastoral minister is designated. The pastor is to carry out for his community the duties of teaching, sanctifying and governing, with the cooperation of other presbyters or deacons and the assistance of lay members of the Christian faithful. In parishes without a resident pastor, the role of the pastoral minister then, is to work very closely with, and follow the guidance of the priest-moderator who supervises the pastoral care given to the parish. The priest supervisor is to provide a mentoring role from his own experience. Regular communication between the priest supervisor and the pastoral minister is essential. Respect and trust are needed for mutual understanding.

The text of canons 528, 529 and 530 provide a list of responsibilities that is all encompassing and impossible to accomplish without collaboration of others. In many situations a pastoral minister is given administration tasks. Our focus here is the sacramental life of the parish without a resident pastor.[33] In particular, we will explore the role of pastoral minister in the areas of ministry of the word, the

---

[32] Canon 519 states: "The pastor (*parochus*) is the proper pastor (*pastor*) of the parish entrusted to him, exercising the pastoral care of the community committed to him under the authority of the diocesan bishop in whose ministry of Christ he has been called to share, so that for the same community he carries out the functions of teaching, sanctifying, and governing, also with the cooperation of other presbyters or deacons and with the assistance of lay members of the Christian faithful, according to the norm of law." *Code of Canon Law*, 170.

[33] See *New Commentary on the Code of Canon Law* (New York/Mahwah: Paulist Press, 2000) 600-700 for cross referencing of specific canons.

21

catechumenate and baptism, Eucharist, marriage and other acts of divine worship.

Canon 528 sets forth the pastor's obligations in general. The canon reads:

> §1. A pastor is obliged to make provision so that the word of God is proclaimed in its entirety to those living in the parish; for this reason, he is to take care that the lay members of the Christian faithful are instructed in the truths of the faith, especially by giving a homily on Sundays and holy days of obligation and by offering catechetical instruction. He is to foster works through which the spirit of the gospel is promoted, even in what pertains to social justice. He is to have particular care for the Catholic education of children and youth. He is to make every effort, even with the collaboration of the Christian faithful, so that the message of the gospel comes also to those who have ceased the practice of their religion or do not profess the true faith. §2. The pastor is to see to it that the Most Holy Eucharist is the center of the parish assembly of the faithful. He is to work so that the Christian faithful are nourished through the devout celebration of the sacraments and, in a special way, that they frequently approach the sacraments of the Most Holy Eucharist and penance. He is also to endeavor that they are led to practice prayer even as families and take part consciously and actively in the sacred liturgy which, under the authority of the diocesan bishop, the pastor must direct in his own parish and is bound to watch over so that no abuses creep in. *Code of Canon Law*, 173.

Canon 529 addresses values a pastor should have. Again the canon states:

> §1. In order to fulfill his office diligently, a pastor is to strive to know the faithful entrusted to his care. Therefore he is to visit families, sharing especially in the cares, anxieties, and griefs of the faithful, strengthening

22

them in the Lord, and prudently correcting them if they are failing in certain areas. With generous love he is to help the sick, particularly those close to death, by refreshing them solicitously with the sacraments and commending their souls to God; with particular diligence he is to seek out the poor, the afflicted, the lonely, those exiled from their country, and similarly those weighted down by special difficulties. He is to work so that spouses and parents are supported in fulfilling their proper duties and is to foster growth of Christian life in the family. §2. A pastor is to recognize and promote the proper part which the lay members of the Christian faithful have in the mission of the Church, by fostering their associations for the purposes of religion. He is to cooperate with his own bishop and the *presbyterium* of the diocese, also working so that the faithful have concern for parochial communion, consider themselves members of the diocese and of the universal Church, and participate in and sustain efforts to promote this same communion. *Code of Canon Law*, 174.

Canon 530 addresses the functions of a pastor:

The following functions are especially entrusted to a pastor: 1° the administration of baptism; 2° the administration of the sacrament of confirmation to those who are in danger of death, according to the norm of can. 883, n. 3; 3° the administration of Viaticum and of the anointing of the sick, without prejudice to the prescript of can. 1003, §§2 and 3, and the imparting of the apostolic blessing; 4° the assistance at marriages and the nuptial blessing; 5° the performance of funeral rites; 6° the blessing of the baptismal font at Easter time, the leading of processions outside the church, and solemn blessing outside the church; 7° the more solemn eucharistic celebration on Sundays and holy days of obligation. *Code of Canon Law*, 174-175.

23

B. Collaboration

Canon 517, §2 states "that participation in the exercise of pastoral care of a parish" is to be entrusted to a deacon or some other person who is not a priest or to a community of persons when the condition of a "dearth of priests" exists.[34] The bishop makes the determination. The code does not specify in detail what particular roles should be given to the pastoral minister. The code simply says that the pastoral minister may be given *that participation in the exercise of the pastoral care of a parish.* The priest possessing the powers and faculties of a pastor "directs" the pastoral care.

Pastoral care is broadly described as teaching, sanctifying and governing in such a manner that parishioners and parish communities will really see that they are members of both the diocese and the universal Church.

In 1997, six congregations and two pontifical councils joined in creating the interdicastral Instruction "On Certain Questions Regarding the Collaboration of the Non-ordained Faithful in the Sacred Ministry of Priest." The congregations were the Congregation for the Clergy, for the Doctrine of the Faith, for Divine Worship and the Discipline of the Sacraments, for Bishops, for the Evangelization of Peoples and for Institutes of Consecrated Life and Societies of Apostolic Life. The pontifical councils were the Pontifical Council for the Laity and for the Interpretation of Legislative Texts. The document promulgated had as its object to outline specific directives to ensure the effective collaboration of the non-ordained while safeguarding the integrity of the pastoral ministry of priests. The document revoked all particular laws, customs and faculties conceded by the Holy See *ad experimentum* or other ecclesiastical authorities which are contrary to the norms it sets. The document emphasizes lay persons may be deputed to participation in ministry for certain offices and roles.

Among the various aspects of the participation of the non-ordained faithful in the Church's mission considered

---

[34] *Code of Canon Law,* 169-170.

by the conciliar documents, that of their direct collaboration with the ministry of the Church's pastors is considered. Indeed, when necessity and expediency in the Church require it, the Pastors, according to established norms from universal law, can entrust to the lay faithful certain offices and roles that are connected to their pastoral ministry but do not require the character of Orders. In this way, it is not one merely of assistance but of mutual enrichment of the common Christian vocation. This collaboration was regulated by successive post-conciliar legislation and particularly by the *Codex Iuris Canonici*.

The code, having referred to the rights and duties of all the faithful, in the subsequent title devoted to the rights and duties of the lay faithful, treats not only of those which are theirs by virtue of their secular condition, but also of those tasks and functions which are not exclusively theirs. Some of these latter refer to any member of the faithful, whether ordained or not, while others are considered along the lines of collaboration with the sacred ministry of cleric. With regard to these last mentioned areas or functions, the non-ordained faithful do not enjoy a right to such tasks and functions. Rather, they are capable of being admitted by the sacred Pastors to those functions which, in accordance with the provisions of law, they can discharge or where ministers are not available they can supply certain of their functions in accordance with the provisions of law.

The document cautioned "only with constant reference to the one source, the 'ministry of Christ' may the term ministry be applied to a certain extent and without ambiguity to the lay faithful: that is, without it being perceived and lived as an undue aspiration to the ordained ministry or as a progressive erosion of is specific nature."

The non-ordained faithful may be generically designated extraordinary ministers when deputed by competent authority to discharge, solely by way of supply, those offices mentions in canon 230, §3[35] and in canons 943 and 1112. Naturally, the concrete term may be applied to those to whom functions are canonically entrusted e.g. catechists, acolytes, lectors, etc. Temporary deputation for liturgical purposes mention in canon 230, §2 does not confer any special or permanent title on the non-ordained faithful.

Collaboration of the deacon or lay person is key to ministry in parishes without a resident pastor.

> Since these tasks are most closely linked to the duties of pastors, (which office requires reception of the sacrament of Orders), it is necessary that all who are in any way involved in this collaboration, exercise particular care to safeguard the nature and mission of sacred ministry and the vocation and secular character of the lay faithful. It must be remembered that "collaboration with" does not, in fact, mean "substitution for."[36]

II. DEACONS AND LAY PERSONS PARTICIPATING IN PASTORAL CARE

The individuals mentioned in canon 517, §2 are a deacon, a lay person, or a community of persons who are not priests. The office for the deacon or lay minister appointed to the pastoral care of a parish in this situation has no official title in the universal law. The section on parishes in the code says very little about the role of deacons and lay persons in parish ministry. The Eastern code does not mention deacons and lay persons as having a share in pastoral care of parishes without a resident pastor but this occurs in Eastern churches when a resident pastor is not available.[37]

---

[35] Cf. Pontifical Council for the Interpretation of Legislative Texts, Response (1 June 1988): *AAS* 80 (1988) 1373.

[36] CFC et al., Instruction: On Certain Questions regarding the Collaboration of the Non-ordained Faithful in the Sacred Ministry of Priest (Washington: United States Catholic Conference, 1997).

[37] John M. Huels, J.C.D., *The Pastoral Companion: A Canon Law Handbook for Catholic Ministry*, (Quincy, IL: Franciscan Press, 2002) 354.

The 2002 Instruction: The Priest, Pastor and Leader of the Parish Community[38] states the preference for the assigning of a deacon in a parish without a resident pastor.

> Where permanent deacons participate in the pastoral care of parishes which, because of shortage of priests, do not have the immediate benefit of a parish priest, they should have precedence over the non-ordained faithful.[39] In virtue of Sacred Orders, the deacon is teacher in so far as he preaches and bears witness to the word of God; he sanctifies when he administers the Sacrament of Baptism, the Holy Eucharist and the sacramentals, he participates at the Holy Eucharist as "a minister of the Blood" and conserves and distributes the Blessed Eucharist; he is a guide in as much as he animates the community or a section of ecclesial life.[40]

The bishop should ensure that lay ministers are prepared to assume the duties given to them.[41] The preparation of lay ministers ought to include completion of a program of theological and pastoral education integrated with spiritual formation. Knowledge of scripture and of canon law as well as the teachings of the Magisterium are to be considered basic qualifications.

It is important that the deacon or lay pastoral minister be given a detailed job description of the rights and obligations of the administration of a parish entrusted to them. Such job descriptions ought to delineate areas of responsibility and define administrative functions.

It is for the bishop to decide whether special authorizations and faculties are to be given. Special authorizations or faculties given to

---

[38] Congregation for Clergy, The Priest, Pastor and Leader of the Parish Community, *L'Osservatore Romano*, English Edition, January 15, 2003.

[39] Congregation for Clergy, Directory for Ministry and Life of Permanent Deacons *Diaconatus Originem* (22 February 1998), n. 41: *AAS* 90 (1998) 901.

[40] Ibid., n. 22: 1.c., 889.

[41] Canon 231, §1 "Lay persons who permanently or temporarily devote themselves to special service of the Church are obliged to acquire the appropriate formation required to fulfill their function properly and to carry out this function conscientiously, eagerly, and diligently." *Code of Canon Law*, 68.

persons who administer a parish in the absence of a resident pastor are found in the *Code of Canon Law* as well as other sources of law such as liturgical books, the Directory for the Application of the Principles and Norms on Ecumenism and other documents from the Holy See. The topic of faculties is very complex.[42] It is to be particularly noted that no one should be granted faculties and authorizations unless they are capable of understanding and using them the way the law intends. Some basic information on faculties in general is given here as introduction.

Faculties grant authorization and powers that person lack in the law. All diocesan faculties and authorizations are granted by the bishop to individuals for the good of the Christian faithful. Diocesan officials, priests, deacons and some lay persons are deputed to act in public ministries in the name of the Church. Without faculties and authorizations the persons act in their own behalf and not in the name of the Church. Huels states the purposes of faculties being granted: (1) to ensure that only qualified persons are assigned to perform certain acts of ministry or administration; (2) to facilitate diocesan and/or parochial administration and the pastoral ministry; and, rarely, (3) to benefit the Church's ministers personally.[43] All diocesan faculties can be divided into acts of power of governance and authorizations for other acts. In general, acts of power of governance can be delegated and subdelegated unless the one granting the faculty has excluded subdelegation. Authorizations for other acts may not be subdelegated with the exception of the faculty to assist at marriages.

Some faculties are granted by the law itself at ordination, by provision of an office and apart from an office. Delegation must be done by one capable and competent to place the act; include those things that essentially constitute the act itself and include the formalities and requirements imposed by the law for the validity of

---

[42] See John M. Huels, J.C.D., *Empowerment for Ministry: A Complete Manual on Diocesan Faculties for Priests, Deacons, and Lay Ministers* for a comprehensive examination of faculties and model.
[43] Ibid., 20.

the act.[44] For validity the faculty granted should be in writing and given each person individually. Both the individual and the diocese should have a record. The faculty should be signed by the bishop in his own hand and should state the extent of their use.

Authorizations that may be granted to the deacon differ from those that may be granted to a lay person. Faculties granted at ordination to the deaconate are noted as such in the text below. It is for the competent authority to grant other authorizations. References to the lay person and authorizations are ones that may be granted depending on the circumstances of the diocese, parish or other community.[45]

Ministry of the Word

The deacon at ordination is granted the faculty to catechize and preach to the faithful apart from the liturgy;[46] to preside at the liturgy of the hours, celebrations of the word, and Sunday celebrations in the absence of a priest where this is permitted; and to preach at the liturgies at which he presides.[47] He may proclaim the gospel at Mass and may give the homily at Mass at the direction of the priest

---

[44] Canon 124, §1 "For the validity of a juridic act it is required that the act is placed by a qualified person and includes those things which essentially constitute the act itself as well as the formalities and requirements imposed by law for the validity of the act. §2. A juridic act placed correctly with respect to its external elements is presumed valid."

Canon 125, §1. "An act placed out of force inflicted on a person from without, which the person was not able to resist in any way, is considered as never to have taken place. §2. An act placed out of grave fear, unjustly inflicted, or out of malice is valid unless the law provides otherwise. It can be rescinded, however, through the sentence of a judge, either at the instance of the injured party or of the party's successors in law, or *ex officio*."

Canon 126 "An act placed out of ignorance or out of error concerning something which constitutes its substance or which amounts to a condition *sine qua non* is invalid. Otherwise it is valid unless the law makes other provision. An act entered into out of ignorance or error, however, can give rise to a rescissory action according to the norm of law." *Code of Canon Law*, 36-37.

[45] See John M. Huels, J.C.D., *Empowerment for Ministry: A Complete Manual on Diocesan Faculties for Priests, Deacons, and Lay Ministers,* 157-190.

[46] Cc. 757 and 762; *Sacrum Diaconatus Ordinem,* 22, 6°.

[47] C. 764; General Instruction of the Liturgy of the Hours, 1971; *Sacrum Diaconatus Ordinem* 22, nn7-8; Directory for Sunday Celebrations in the Absence of a Priest, (Congregation for Divine Worship), June 2, 1988.

celebrant.[48]

The lay person may preside at liturgies of the word apart from the Eucharistic celebration, penitential celebrations apart from the sacrament of penance, and the liturgy of the hours. If the lay person will be absent, he or she may subdelegate this faculty to another suitably instructed layperson.[49] On Sundays and holy days of obligation, the lay person may preside at the liturgy of the word, morning prayer at which holy communion is distributed in accord with the approved rite.[50] This may be done only for the benefit of the faithful who are unable to go to another church for the Eucharist; it may not be done more than once a day in any one place or when Mass is celebrated there that day.[51] With the permission of the priest supervisor, the lay person may subdelegate this faculty when he or she is absent, but only to a person who has been suitably instructed. It belongs to the diocesan bishop, after hearing the presbyteral council, to decide whether Sunday assemblies without the celebration of the Eucharist should be held regularly in his diocese.[52]

The lay person may preach in the parish church [in keeping with the policy on lay preaching of the conference of bishops and/or the diocese] and at all liturgical celebrations at which he or she lawfully presides.[53] The lay person may read a homily prepared by the priest supervisor.[54] The lay person may preach the word of God apart from the liturgy. Preaching outside a church or oratory requires no

[48] General Instruction of the Roman Missal, 3rd edition (2000) 174, 171c.

[49] Cc. 230, §3, and 1174, §2; General Instruction of the Roman Missal, 3rd edition (2000) 258.

[50] In the USA, the approved ritual book is *Sunday Celebrations in the Absence of a Priest: Leader's Edition* (New York: The Catholic Book Publishing Company, 1994). In Canada, the approved rites are found in *Sunday Celebration of the Word and Hours* (Ottawa: CCCB, 1995).

[51] Congregation for Divine Worship, Directory for Sunday Celebrations in the Absence of a Priest, translated by the International Committee on English in the Liturgy (Washington: United States Catholic Conference, 1988) n. 24; *Ecclesiae de mysterio*, Instruction on Certain Questions Concerning the Cooperation of the Lay Faithful in the Ministry of Priests, (Congregation for the Clergy et al.), August 15, 1997 article 7.

[52] Ibid.

[53] C. 766; *Ecclesiae de mysterio*, Instruction on Certain Questions Concerning the Cooperation of the Lay Faithful in the Ministry of Priests, (Congregation for the Clergy et al.), August 15, 1997 article 2.

[54] Directory for Sunday Celebrations in the Absence of a Priest, Congregation for Divine Worship (June 2, 1988) n. 43.

faculty. The lay person may not preach at Mass. With permission of the presiding priest, the lay person may give a brief instruction or personal testimony by way of explanation of the homily given by the priest or speak as part of a dialogue homily.[55]

The Catechumenate and Baptism

The deacon at ordination is granted the faculty to administer baptism to infants – those under seven and those lacking the use of reason.[56] To deacons serving in parishes, the bishop may grant the faculty to confer infant baptism in a private house for a grave reason that makes it difficult or dangerous for the infant to be brought to the church.[57]

John M. Huels in *Empowerment for Ministry* recommends deacon pastoral administrators be granted two pagellae. One with the faculties given to all deacons and those serving in parishes, and one with any additional faculties.

> The most important consideration in granting special faculties to deacon pastoral administrators is the involvement of the priest who supervises the pastoral care of the parish (priest supervisor). Sometimes, the priest supervisor is a retired priest or a priest who has one or more apostolates elsewhere; he has responsibility for only minimal pastoral care in the parish. Mainly, he celebrates the sacraments that require presbyteral orders, but he does little else that could be done by the deacon administrator. In that case, the faculties granted the deacon should be as wide as possible, matching those that would be given to the pastor of a parish, to the extent permitted by law and the ability of the deacon. However, if the priest supervisor has greater time to

---

[55] *Ecclesiae de mysterio*, Instruction on Certain Questions Concerning the Cooperation of the Lay Faithful in the Ministry of Priests, (Congregation for the Clergy et al.), August 15, 1997 article 3 §§ 2-3.

[56] C. 861, §1.

[57] C. 860, §1; *Rite of Baptism of Children*, 2nd ed., 1973, n, 12.

devote to overseeing the pastoral care of the parish, even if not resident there, the need for some faculties in section four will be less.[58]

The bishop may grant some or all of the additional faculties below to the deacon serving in pastoral administration of a parish.

The deacon may depute catechists, truly worthy and properly prepared, to celebrate the minor exorcism of the catechumenate and the blessings of the catechumens when a priest or deacon cannot be present.[59] The deacon may permit the simple rite for the initiation of an adult in the exceptional circumstances envisioned in the law, namely, sickness, old age, change of residence, long absence for travel, or a depth of Christian conversion and degree of religious maturity in the catechumen. In all other cases, the permission of the diocesan bishop is necessary to use the abbreviated rite.[60] The deacon may dispense from one scrutiny for a serious reason or, in extraordinary circumstances, even from two. The extraordinary circumstances for granting the dispensation from two scrutinies are the exceptional circumstances in permitting the simple rite of initiation. For pastoral reasons, in particular circumstances, the deacon may invite a minister of another church or ecclesial community to take part in the celebration of baptism by reading a lesson, offering a prayer, or the like. The actual baptism is to be celebrated by the Catholic minister alone.[61]

The lay person may celebrate the minor exorcisms of the catechumenate and the blessings of catechumens.[62] The lay person may use the abbreviated catechumenate in the exceptional circum-

---

[58] John M. Huels, J.C.D., *Empowerment for Ministry: A Complete Manual on Diocesan Faculties for Priests, Deacons, and Lay Ministers.* (New York/Mahwah: Paulist Press, 2003) 165-171.

[59] *Ordo initiationis christianae adultorum,* editio typica, 1972, n. 44, 48, 109, 119; *Rite of Christian Initiation of Adults* 1989 (USA) and 1987 (Canada) n. 12, 16, 91, 97.

[60] C. 851, 1°; *Ordo initiationis christianae adultorum,* editio typical, 1972, n 240, 274; *Rite of Christian Initiation of Adults* 1989 (USA) 331-332, and 1987 (Canada) 307-308.

[61] Directory for the Application of the Principles and Norms on Ecumenism (Pontifical Council for Promoting Christian Unity), 1993, n. 97.

[62] *Ordo initiationis christianae adultorum,* editio typical, 1972, n. 44, 48, 109, 119; *Rite of Christian Initiation of Adults* n. 12, 16, 91, 97.

stances envisioned in the law, namely, sickness, old age, change of residence, long absence for travel, or a depth of Christian conversion and degree of religious maturity in the catechumen. In all other cases, the permission of the diocesan bishop is necessary to use the abbreviated process.[63] Apart from danger of death, in individual instances, the lay person may celebrate infant baptism only if one of the following conditions applies: (1) a priest or deacon has already scheduled the baptism, but he is unable to come and another priest or deacon is not available; or (2) no priest or deacon can celebrate the baptism within four weeks after the child's birth.[64] Under the same circumstances, the lay person may confer infant baptism in a private house for a grave reason that makes it difficult or dangerous for the infant to be brought to the church.[65] The lay person may not celebrate the baptism of anyone seven years of age or older with the use of reason, except in danger of death when a priest is unavailable, since the presbyter who baptizes must administer confirmation at the time of adult baptism. For pastoral reasons, in particular circumstances, the lay person may invite a minister of another church or ecclesial community to take part in the celebration of baptism by reading a lesson, offering a prayer, or the like. The actual baptism is to be celebrated by the Catholic minister alone. This can only be done with the consent of the priest or deacon who celebrates the baptism unless it is with the faculties above on infant baptism in danger of death and baptism in a private house.

Eucharist

The deacon is granted at ordination the faculty to assist the presiding priest at Mass and other liturgical celebrations as indicated in the rites.[66] The deacon may administer the blood of Christ at Mass or, when communion is given only under the species bread,

---

[63] C. 851, 1°; *Ordo initiationis christianae adultorum*, editio typical, 1972, n 240, 274; *Rite of Christian Initiation of Adults* 1989 (USA) 331-332, and 1987 (Canada) 307-308.

[64] *Ecclesiae de mysterio*, Instruction on Certain Questions Concerning the Cooperation of the Lay Faithful in the Ministry of Priests, (Congregation for the Clergy et al.), August 15, 1997 article 11.

[65] C. 860, §1; *Rite of Baptism of Children*, 2nd ed., 1973, n, 12.

[66] *Sacrum Diaconatus Ordinem*, 22, 1°.

the body of Christ.[67] The deacon may preside at the Rite of Distributing Holy Communion Outside Mass, and bring holy communion to the sick and infirm.[68] The deacon may preside at benediction and give the blessing with the reserved Eucharist.[69] The deacon granted the faculty may appoint a qualified person to distribute holy communion for single occasions when you are presiding at a communion service and there are too many communicants and insufficient ordinary and extraordinary ministers of communion or when bringing Viaticum to a dying person is necessary and no ordinary or extraordinary minister is available.[70] In the absence of a priest, deacon, acolyte or extraordinary minister of communion, the deacon may appoint, in individual instances, appoint a lay person to expose publicly the Eucharist for the adoration of the faithful and afterward to repose it.[71] When no priest is available to celebrate Mass, and neither the deacon nor another deacon is available for the Sunday celebration of the word or liturgy of the hours, the deacon may appoint a suitably instructed lay minister, approved by the bishop for this function, to take his place using the appropriate rite.[72]

The lay person may distribute holy communion outside Mass to the sick, infirm, and aged who cannot come to church. Whenever Mass cannot be celebrated on a weekday or Sunday, the lay person may distribute holy communion at the liturgy of the word or the liturgy of the hours. The lay person may distribute holy communion under either species during Mass when necessary.[73] In the absence of a priest or deacon, the lay person may expose publicly the Eucharist

---

[67] C. 910, §1; *General Instruction of the Roman Missal*, n. 182.

[68] *Rite of Holy Communion and Worship of the Eucharist Outside Mass*, 17, 26; *Pastoral Care of the Sick: Rites of Anointing and Viaticum*, 81-96.

[69] C. 943.

[70] C. 230, §3 and *Ecclesiae de mysterio*, Instruction on Certain Questions Concerning the Cooperation of the Lay Faithful in the Ministry of Priests, (Congregation for the Clergy et al.), August 15, 1997 article 8, §1.

[71] *Rite of Holy Communion and Worship of the Eucharist Outside Mass*, 91-92.

[72] Directory for Sunday Celebrations in the Absence of a Priest (Congregation of Divine Worship), June 2, 1988, 24 and *Ecclesiae de mysterio*, Instruction on Certain Questions Concerning the Cooperation of the Lay Faithful in the Ministry of Priests, (Congregation for the Clergy et al.), August 15, 1997 article 7.

[73] Cc. 230, §3; 910, §2 and *Ecclesiae de mysterio*, Instruction on Certain Questions Concerning the Cooperation of the Lay Faithful in the Ministry of Priests, (Congregation for the Clergy et al.), August 15, 1997 article 8.

for the adoration of the faithful and repose it afterwards. Only a priest or deacon may give the benediction.[74] Special mandate from the bishop is necessary for parishes without a resident pastor where the need for Sunday celebrations is ongoing.

Marriage

The deacon who is granted the faculty may, within the territory of the parish, validly assist at marriages involving at least one party who is a Catholic of the Latin church.[75] The faculty may be used only within the territory of the parish within the limits of the pastoral charge. Whether this faculty is granted or not is determined by the bishop and depends on the aptitude of the deacon. Whenever an impediment is discovered after everything has already been prepared for the wedding, and the marriage cannot be delayed without probable danger of grave harm until a dispensation is obtained from the competent authority, the deacon may dispense in occult cases from all impediments except prior bond, impotence, consanguinity in the direct line and the second degree of the collateral line, sacred orders, and a public perpetual vow of chastity in a religious institute of pontifical right. The deacon may dispense either Catholic party, even if they live outside the parish territory, provided the marriage takes place in the parish and may dispense parishioners even if the marriage is lawfully celebrated outside the parish territory. This faculty is granted to deacons by law, provided they have the faculty to assist at marriage.[76]

The deacon granted the faculty to assist at marriage, after the conditions of canon 1125 have been fulfilled, may, for a just and reasonable cause, permit a mixed marriage between a Latin Catholic and a baptized non-Catholic to be celebrated in the parish, provided there is no doubt about the validity of the baptism of the Catholic party.[77] Upon the request of the couple, if the deacon has the faculty

---

[74] C. 943; *Rite of Holy Communion and Worship of the Eucharist Outside Mass*, 91-92.
[75] Cc.1108; 1111.
[76] C. 1080, §1.
[77] C. 1124.

to assist at marriage, even by special delegation, may invite the minister of the party of the other church or ecclesial community to participate in the celebration of the marriage by reading from scripture, giving a brief exhortation, and/or blessing the couple.[78]

The deacon granted the faculty to assist at marriage, may permit: (1) the marriage of transients (*vagi*), provided the diocesan marriage preparation program is observed to the extent possible, and baptismal certificates or sworn affidavits show they are free to marry; (2) the marriage of a person who is bound by a natural obligation toward another party or children arising from a previous union, provided these obligations are being fulfilled; and (3) the marriage of a Catholic with another Catholic who has notoriously rejected the faith, provided the norms of canon 1125 have been observed.[79] The deacon may permit a parishioner to be married in another Catholic church or oratory.[80] The permission should be in writing and a copy retained for the archives. If the deacon has general delegation to assist at marriage, he already has the power by law to subdelegate the faculty to another cleric in individual instances. In a case of necessity when the deacon is unable to assist at a marriage, if no other cleric is available, may grant special delegation to a lay substitute, previously approved by the bishop, or to a lay minister from another parish who has been appointed by the diocesan bishop for this ministry.

As an extraordinary minister, the lay person granted the faculty to assist at marriages may, provided at least one party is Latin Catholic or is a catechumen who intends to become a Catholic of the Latin church. This faculty may be licitly used with at least the presumed permission of the priest supervisor.[81] In individual cases, when the local ordinary or priest supervisor cannot be reached, the lay person may grant special delegation to another priest or deacon to assist at

---

[78] Pontifical Council for Promoting Christian Unity, Directory for the Application of the Principles and Norms on Ecumenism, March 25, 1993, (Vatican City/Washington: United States Catholic Conference, 1993).

[79] C. 1071, §1, nn. 1, 3, 4; §2.

[80] C. 1118, §1.

[81] C. 1112, §1 and *Ecclesiae de mysterio*, Instruction on Certain Questions Concerning the Cooperation of the Lay Faithful in the Ministry of Priests, (Congregation for the Clergy et al.), August 15, 1997 article 10.

marriage. In necessity, when the lay person is unable to be present and no cleric is available, and when unable to reach the diocesan bishop, the lay person may grant special delegation to a lay substitute, previously approved by the bishop or to a lay minister from another parish whom the diocesan bishop has appointed for this ministry. At mixed marriages in the parish church, when the couple requests it, the lay person may invite the minister of the party of the other church or ecclesial community to participate in the celebration of marriage, to read from the scriptures, to give a brief exhortation, and/or to bless the couple.[82]

Other Acts of Divine Worship

The deacon may preside at benediction and give the blessing with the reserved Eucharist.[83] The deacon may celebrate the minor exorcisms and blessings of catechumens.[84] The deacon may give the blessings of the rites at which he presides; he may preside at other blessings in accord with the *Book of Blessings*.[85] The deacon may preside at penitential celebrations when the sacrament of penance is not celebrated.[86] The deacon may celebrate the rites for visits to the sick and the prayers on the occasion of death.[87] When a priest is not available, the deacon may preside at funeral rites – the vigil, funeral liturgy outside Mass, and committal.[88] When a priest is unavailable, the deacon may celebrate the funeral liturgy in the presence of the cremated remains of a deceased person, taking into

---

[82] Directory for the Application of the Principles and Norms on Ecumenism (Pontifical Council for Promoting Christian Unity), 1993.

[83] C. 943.

[84] *Rite of Christian Initiation of Adults*, 1988 (USA) and 1987 (Canada); *Ordo initiationis christianae adultorum*, editio typica 1972

[85] *Rituale Romanum: De Benedictionibus*, editio typica 1984 and *Book of Blessings* (New York: Catholic Book Publishing Company, 1989), 1987 International Commission on English in the Liturgy, Washington, DC.

[86] Rite of Penance, 1973.

[87] *Ordo unctionis infirmorum eorumque pastoralis curae*, editio typica 1972, nn. 138, 151; *Pastoral Care of the Sick: Rites of Anointing and Viaticum*, 1983, nn. 212, 221.

[88] *Ordo exsequiarum*, editio typica 1969 and *Order of Christian Funerals*, (Washington 1985) International Commission on English in the Liturgy, 1986 (Canada) and (New York: Catholic Publishing Company, 1989) (USA).

account the concrete circumstances in each individual case and always observing the following conditions: (1) There is no anti-Christian motive for choosing cremation.[89] (2) The cremated remains will be handled with respect and buried or entombed in a place reserved for this purpose. (3) There is no other canonical prohibition of a funeral liturgy, namely, for notorious apostates, heretics, and schismatics and other manifest sinners for whom ecclesiastical funerals cannot be granted without public scandal to the faithful.[90] Doubtful cases are to be referred to the bishop. The deacon may celebrate or impart other sacramentals in accord with the law.[91]

The deacon may permit competent lay ministers and catechists to celebrate blessings from the *Book of Blessings* that are not reserved to a priest or deacon, provided sufficient clergy or instituted acolytes and readers are unavailable.[92] The deacon may permit church funeral rites for children who died before baptism, provided their parents had intended to have them baptized.[93] The deacon may celebrate the Church's funeral rites for a validly baptized member of another church or ecclesial community, provided this would not be contrary to the wishes of the deceased person and provided the minister of the deceased person is unavailable.[94]

In individual cases and for a just cause, the deacon may dispense parishioners anywhere they are and others who are in the parish territory from the obligations to attend Mass and abstain from work on Sundays and holy days of obligation, or he may commute the obligation to another pious work. Under the same conditions the deacon may dispense from or commute the obligations of fast and abstinence on a day of penance.[95] The deacon may dispense from private vows, provided the dispensation does not injure the acquired

---

[89] C. 1176, §3.

[90] C. 1184.

[91] Cc. 1168; 1169, §3.

[92] *Rituale Romanum: De Benedictionibus*, editio typica 1984 and *Book of Blessings*, 1987 International Commission on English in the Liturgy, Washington, DC. N.18d.

[93] C. 1183, §2.

[94] C. 1183, §3; Directory for the Application of the Principles and Norms on Ecumenism (Pontifical Council for Promoting Christian Unity), 1993.

[95] C. 1245.

rights of others. The deacon may dispense from promissory oaths, unless dispensation from an oath would tend to harm one or other persons who refuse to remit its obligation. The deacon may commute the obligation of a private vow or oath to a lesser good. This faculty may be used on behalf of parishioners wherever they are staying and within the boundaries of the parish on behalf of visitors.[96]

The lay person may celebrate blessings from the *Book of Blessings* that are not reserved to a priest or deacon. The local ordinary may grant this faculty to lay persons after ascertaining their proper pastoral formation and prudence in the apostolate. The lay person may preside at penitential celebrations when the sacrament of penance is not celebrated.[97] The lay person may celebrate the rites for visits to the sick and say the prayers on the occasion of death.[98] On Ash Wednesday, the lay person may administer ashes previously blessed by the priest supervisor or another priest or deacon.[99]

The lay person may celebrate the funeral rites of the Church – the vigil, the funeral liturgy outside Mass, and the rite of committal – for deceased parishioners, including a catechumen, and for non-parishioners, if this was requested by them before death or by the person in charge of the funeral arrangements.[100] This faculty may be granted by the diocesan bishop where this is permitted by decree of the conference of bishops or by indult of the Holy See.

A lay person may celebrate funeral rites for children who died before baptism, provided their parents had intended to have them

---

[96] Cc. 1196, 1°; 1203.

[97] Rite of Penance, 1973, nn. 36, 37.

[98] *Ordo unctionis infirmorum eorumque pastoralis curae*, editio typica 1972, nn. 138, 151 and *Pastoral Care of the Sick: Rites of Anointing and Viaticum*, 1983, nn. 212, 221

[99] *Book of Blessings*, 1987 International Commission on English in the Liturgy, Washington, DC. N.1659.

[100] *Order of Christian Funerals*, n. 14 1985 International Commission on English in the Liturgy, Washington, DC. 1986 (Canada) and 1989 (USA); *Ordo exsequiarum*, edtitio typica 1969; *Ecclesiae de mysterio*, Instruction on Certain Questions Concerning the Cooperation of the Lay Faithful in the Ministry of Priests, (Congregation for the Clergy et al.), August 15, 1997 article 12; c. 1177, §2.

baptized.[101] A lay person may celebrate the Church's funeral rites for a validly baptized member of another church or ecclesial community, provided this would not be contrary to the wishes of the deceased person and provided the minister of the deceased person is unavailable.[102] A lay person may celebrate the funeral liturgy in the presence of the cremated remains of a deceased person, taking into account the concrete circumstances in each individual case, and always observing the following conditions: (1) There is no anti-Christian motive for choosing cremation.[103] (2) The cremated remains will be handled with respect and buried or entombed in a place reserved for this purpose. (3) There is no other canonical prohibition of a funeral liturgy, namely, for notorious apostates, heretics, and schismatics and other manifest sinners for whom ecclesiastical funerals cannot be granted without public scandal to the faithful.[104] Doubtful cases are to be referred to the bishop.[105]

Selected Faculties in Danger of Death

A deacon has the following faculties from ordination. These faculties may be used only if someone is in danger of death. If a priest is unavailable, a deacon may baptize anyone not yet validly baptized, including a fetus, provided the person is alive.[106] Those who had the use of reason at any time during their life may not be baptized without having manifested this intention. They must also have some knowledge of the principal truths of the faith and must promise to observe the commandments of the Christian religion.[107] A deacon may celebrate the Rite of Viaticum Outside Mass, except the apostolic pardon, with at least the presumed permission of the

[101] C. 1183, §2.
[102] C. 1183, §3, Directory for the Application of the Principles and Norms on Ecumenism (Pontifical Council for Promoting Christian Unity), 1993.
[103] C. 1176, §3.
[104] C. 1184.
[105] See NCCB, *Order of Christian Funerals*, Appendix: Cremation, 426 and CCCB, *Order of Christian Funerals*, (New York: Catholic Book Publishing Company, 1989), Appendix IV: Cremation, in National Bulletin on Liturgy 26 (1993) 29.
[106] Cc. 861, §2; 868, §2; and 871.
[107] C. 865, §2.

pastor, chaplain, or superior, who must be notified afterwards. He may also give Viaticum to a baptized non-Catholic who is in danger of death.[108] A deacon may celebrate the Rite of Commendation of the Dying.[109]

Even if he lacks the faculty to assist at marriage, when one or both parties is in danger of death and when the local ordinary cannot be reached, a deacon may dispense the parties to marriage both from the form to be observed in the celebration of marriage and from every impediment of ecclesiastical law, whether public or occult, except the impediment arising from the sacred order of the presbyterate.[110]

If a priest or deacon is unavailable, a lay person may baptize anyone not yet validly baptized, including a fetus, provided the person is alive.[111] Normally a priest should baptize in danger of death so that he can confirm the person immediately.[112] A lay person may celebrate the Rite of Viaticum Outside Mass, except the parts reserved to a priest or a deacon, with at least the presumed permission of the pastor, chaplain, or superior, who must be notified afterwards.[113] A lay person may also give Viaticum to a baptized non-Catholic who is in danger of death, in accord with the law. A lay person may celebrate the Rite of Commendation of the Dying.[114]

When one or both parties is in urgent danger of death and when the local ordinary and the priest supervisor cannot be reached, a lay person may dispense the parties to marriage both from the form to be observed in the celebration of marriage and from every impediment of ecclesiastical law, whether public or occult, except the

---

[108] *Pastoral Care of the Sick: Rites of Anointing and Viaticum*, 1983, nn. 197-211; c. 911, §2 and c. 844, §§3-4.

[109] *Ordo unctionis infirmorum eorumque pastoralis curae*, editio typica 1972, nn. 142; and ibid., nn. 165, 212, 222.

[110] C. 1079, §2.

[111] C. 865, §2.

[112] C. 866.

[113] C. 911; *Pastoral Care of the Sick: Rites of Anointing and Viaticum*, 1983, nn. 197-211; c. 911, §2 and c. 844, §§3-4.

[114] *Ordo unctionis infirmorum eorumque pastoralis curae*, editio typica 1972, nn. 142; and *Pastoral Care of the Sick: Rites of Anointing and Viaticum*, 1983, nn. 165, 212, 222.

impediment arising from the sacred order of the presbyterate.[115] The faculty may be used: (1) for a marriage in the territory of the parish; (2) out-side the parish, when either party is a parishioner. The faculty is intended only for an emergency so the person may die in peace in a valid marriage.

Sacramental Preparation

The Christian faithful have the right to spiritual assistance from their pastors. The right is established in canon 213 which states "The Christian faithful have the right to receive assistance from the sacred pastors out of the spiritual goods of the Church, especially the word of God and the sacraments." Although this canon applies primarily to the Christian faithful in full communion with the Catholic Church (c. 205), canon 844, §§3-4 extends the reception of the three sacraments of penance, Eucharist, and anointing of the sick to members of the Eastern churches and other Christians who do not have full communion with the Catholic Church under certain restrictions.

Canon 834 establishes a basic principle for understanding spiritual assistance by describing the sacred liturgy through which the Church fulfills the priestly function (*munus*) of Jesus Christ. According to canon 839, the function of sanctifying includes the sacraments, prayer, works of penance and charity, and pious exercises in addition to liturgy and public worship. The sacraments "contribute in the greatest way to establish, strengthen, and manifest ecclesiastical communion" (c. 840); therefore, sacred pastors are obliged to provide for adequate preparation for their reception (c. 843, §2) and not to deny the sacraments "to those who seek them at appropriate times, are properly disposed, and are not prohibited by law from receiving them" (c. 843, §1).

Only the person can truly know whether they seek the sacrament with the proper disposition. There is no pastoral duty to assess the faith of the person. Although a judgment of whether the person is of

---

[115] C. 1079, §2.

the proper disposition can and sometimes must be made by the minister, the canon establishes a presumption in favor of the Christian person.

The duty of canon 843 is for the pastoral ministers to provide preparation to assist the person.

> Because the law imposes a duty on pastors of souls and other members of the faithful to provide sacramental preparation, there is an implied right of the faithful to have access to this preparation. The burden of the law does not fall on the faithful. The law does not say that they must have such preparation before they can receive a sacrament. The law imposes the duty on the Church's ministers to provide this preparation.[116]

The faithful have the right to preparation for the sacraments. It does not follow that they may be denied the sacraments because they have not had such preparation.

Infant Baptism (cc. 851, 2°; 868, §1)

Canon 851, 2° uses general terms of the preparation of parents and sponsors.

> The celebration of baptism must be prepared properly; consequently: the parents of an infant to be baptized and those who are to undertake the function of sponsor are to be instructed properly on the meaning of this sacrament and the obligations attached to it. The pastor personally or through others is to take care that the parents are properly instructed through both pastoral advice and common prayer, bringing several families together and, where possible, visiting them.

---

[116] John M. Huels, J.C.D., "Preparation for the Sacraments: Faith, Rights," *Studia Canonica* 28 (1994) 33-58.

As a general rule, the parents and sponsors should take part in the program of preparation offered at the parish. The law does not require attendance at a program. It uses exhortative language to set forth the best way of doing the preparation. In cases where parents or sponsors are unable to attend a catechetical program of the parish, the pastor or lay minister can judge whether the reason given by the parents is sufficient to excuse them.

Canon 868 states there must be a "founded hope" that the child will be raised in the Catholic faith. Most parents, even if they do not regularly practice their faith, have at least some minimal faith themselves and desire baptism for their child. They should be invited and encouraged to do so but the minister can delay the sacrament only for the reasons given in the law i.e., consent not given by at least one parent and if a founded hope the child will be raised Catholic is "altogether lacking." Then, baptism is being deferred not denied. The minister must tell the parents under what conditions baptism can later be granted.

Confirmation (c. 889, §2)

Canon law considers young children to be fit subjects for confirmation. It imposes minimal requirements for reception of the sacrament. Canon 889, §2 states "to receive confirmation licitly outside the danger of death requires that a person who has the use of reason be suitably instructed, properly disposed, and able to renew the baptismal promises."

The proper disposition to receive confirmation includes being in the state of grace.[117] The minister can presume sufficient disposition in young children and adults who have been given instruction, including an admonition they are to be in the state of grace. Some instruction is ordinarily required before confirmation. The law does not require a lengthy program of instruction, retreats, service projects or other specific means of catechesis. It only requires instruction suitable to the level of the young child. Failure to participate in or

---

[117] *Rite of Confirmation*, 12.

complete a parish program of instruction cannot be used as the sole reason for refusing the sacrament.

First Penance and First Communion (cc. 913-914)

Canon 913, §1 requires that persons "have sufficient knowledge and careful preparation so that they understand the mystery of Christ according to their capacity and are able to receive the body of the Christ with faith and devotion." The appropriate time for the celebration of first communion is at the age of reason which in the law is presumed to be about the age of seven (c. 97, §2). Canon 914 is directed to parents and pastors. It obliges them to see that children who have reached the use of reason receive holy communion as early as possible.

It is important to recognize that parents are not required by canon law to participate in sacramental preparation programs. It is a good formative practice but a child cannot be denied holy communion, penance or confirmation based on parental non-participation. This is a violation of the child's right to the sacraments.

Some preparation for the sacraments of first penance and first Eucharist is necessary if a child is to be admitted to these sacraments. It is helpful for pastors and lay ministers to realize that parents have the right and obligation to be the primary educators of children in the faith (c. 226, §2). A specific program of catechetical preparation is not required. Exceptions to parish programs should be permitted when there are good reasons. Adequate preparation can be provided by the parents or someone else willing to undertake the responsibility.

Some families are not registered in any parish because they have no domicile or quasi-domicile. For legal purposes, the parish of those who do not have a domicile or quasi-domicile is whatever parish they are staying in at the time (c. 107, §2). A baptized Catholic child of such parents can and should be admitted to the sacraments of confirmation, Eucharist and penance in the parish where they are staying. Some minimal instruction would be needed so they are able to understand the meaning of the sacraments according to their capacity and celebrate and receive them properly.

Marriage (cc. 1063-1067)

As part of preparation for marriage, canon law strongly recommends that they approach the sacraments of penance and the holy Eucharist so that they are in a state of grace when they marry (c. 1065, §2). Canon 1063 is the principal canon devoted to the topic of marriage preparation. It is addressed to pastors and pastoral ministers and obliges them to see that formation in Christian marriage is provided in four ways: (1) through preaching, catechetical instruction, and the means of social communication in order to teach about the meaning of Christian marriage; (2) through the more immediate personal preparation of the engaged couple: (3) through the fruitful celebration of the marriage liturgy; and (4) through continuing assistance given to married couples.

The code leaves it to local Churches – to the conferences of bishops (c. 1067) and to dioceses (cc. 1064; 1077) to develop more specific policies regulating marriage preparation. Canon 1077, §1 is the legal basis for those marriage preparation programs that permit the delay of marriage in cases where couples lack the necessary disposition or readiness.

If marriage preparation programs are mandatory it is important they be done well. Even mandatory programs should admit of exceptions for people who cannot attend the classes. Local policies must be flexible enough to accommodate the genuine needs of persons.

We must remember the Holy Spirit who acts through the sacraments to "give growth and healing to Christ's members."[118] As ministers we serve best when we facilitate persons coming to the Church for this growth and healing.

---

[118] *The Catechism of the Catholic Church,* (New York/Mahwah: Paulist Press, 1994) article 798.

Liturgy of the Hours

The celebration of the Liturgy of the Hours can provide a means of communal prayer. It is a complementary way to call forth the devotions of the People of God, especially adoration and worship of the Blessed Sacrament.

Canon 276, §1, 3° states "priests and deacons aspiring to the presbyterate are obliged to carry out the liturgy of the hours daily according to the proper and approved liturgical books; permanent deacons, however, are to carry out the same to the extent defined by the conference of bishops."

The conciliar document *Sacrosanctum Concilium* imposed on bishops, priests and deacons the juridic obligation of fulfilling daily the liturgy of the hours. The celebration of the Liturgy of the Hours is meant to provide a means that the whole course of the day and night praise is given to God.

> The Liturgy of the Hours is intended to become the prayer of the whole People of God. In it Christ himself continues his priestly work through the Church. His members participate according to their own place in the Church and the circumstances of their lives: priests devoted to the pastoral ministry, because they are called to remain diligent in prayer and the service of the word; religious, by the charism of their consecrated lives; all the faithful as much as possible: pastors of souls should see to it that the principal hours, especially Vespers, are celebrated in common in church on Sundays and on the more solemn feasts. The laity, too, are encouraged to recite the divine office, either with the priests, or among themselves, or even individually.[119]

---

[119] Ibid., article 1175.

The celebration of the Liturgy of the Hours can provide a means of communal prayer. It is a complementary way to call forth the devotions of the People of God, especially adoration and worship of the Blessed Sacrament.

Appendix A

Sample Application form for Position of
Parish Life Coordinator

Arch/Diocese of _____

Name _____

Address _____

_____

Telephone _____

Religious Community (if applicable) _____

Education
Degree	*Year*	*Educational Institutions*	*Major Field*

Work Experience
Dates	*Position*	*Place*	*Contact Person*

Professional Involvement/Continuing Education
Date	Place	Description

Please include with this application the following documentation:

1. Sacramental records
2. Letter of recommendation from Pastor
3. Statement of interest in and understanding of the position of Parish Life Coordinator
4. Statement of support from spouse/religious superior (as applicable)
5. List of references

Appendix B

Sample Contract: Parish Lay Employment Agreement

In this sample contract, the parish is identified as the employer of the parish life coordinator. It is a standard parish employee contract and exemplifies "at will" employment agreements. Civil counsel should be consulted for applicable civil norms and advice before a diocese determines the form of contract to be utilized with a parish life coordinator.

Arch/Diocese of _____

Parish Lay Employment Agreement

This agreement is made and entered into in the State of _____, County of _____, this _____ day of _____, 20 __ between the parish of _____, hereafter referred to as "employer" and (*parish life coordinator*), hereafter referred to as "employee."

1. *Nature of Agreement*

The employer hereby employs the employee as parish life coordinator for the parish of _____. Employee agrees to perform faithfully, industriously and ethically to the best of the employee's ability, experience, Catholic religious training and talents those duties set forth in the job description attached as "Exhibit A" hereto and initialed by the parties and made part of this agreement. Employee agrees to perform those duties at the times and places specified by the employer.

2. *Duration*

Unless sooner terminated in accordance with the provision of paragraph 5 below, this agreement and the employee's rights, duties and responsibilities shall commence as of the _____ day of _____, 20___ and shall terminate on the _____ day of _____, 20____.

3. *Compensation and Benefits*

a) Employee shall receive full payment of all services to be performed under this contract a mutually agreed sum of _____ per _____ which shall be paid to employee in equal biweekly installments subject to all legal and contractual deductions including those for and by federal and state laws and regulations.

b) Employee shall also receive, during the term of this agreement, all other benefits including medical and hospitalization insurance coverage as provided for lay employees of the Arch/diocese of ___ _____ Employee Handbook and which said benefits are subject to changed, modification or reduction from time to time within the discretion of the Arch/diocese of _____.

4. *Automobile Expenses and Insurance*

a) If the employee is to use his or her automobile in the course of the employee's work, the employer shall reimburse employee for the use of his or her private automobile at the rate which from time to time is currently being reimbursed to employees and clergy of the Arch/diocese of _____ for travel associated with employee's work excluding regular travel to and from work.

b) Employee shall obtain and maintain during the existence of this agreement, liability insurance on the automobile he or she uses to perform the duties set forth in the job description annexed hereto. That insurance shall contain such minimal limits of liability as are required by the Arch/diocese of _____ from time to time and verification thereof shall be given to the employer in writing.

c) Employer shall reimburse employee for travel expenses, including meals and lodging away from residence, provided such expenses are associated with his or her work, are approved by the employer in advance of the expenditures and appropriate receipts of expenditures are submitted to employer.

5. *Termination*

a) This agreement shall be terminated by either employer or employee without cause and for any reason upon thirty days advance written notice to the employee. Upon termination all terms and conditions of this agreement for cause shall include but not be limited to the following:

1) failure to comply with the terms of this agreement or the policies and procedures of the employer;

2) incompetence, neglect of duty, immorality, default of character, public scandal or other circumstances that would render employee unsuitable for continued employment;

3) inability of the employee, for whatever reason, to perform the essential functions of his or her assigned duties at the times and places specified by the employer for a period of at least forty-five (45) consecutive days or more than sixty (60) days in the aggregate in any twelve (12) months period from the date of this agreement.

6. *Renewal*

This agreement shall be automatically renewed for an additional period of one (1) year, commencing on the day following the completion of the term of this agreement as set forth in paragraph 2 except and unless on or before the first day of April of each year either party hereto shall notify the other party hereto of his or her intention not to renew the agreement for the ensuing term. If the agreement is not signed by April 15, it is understood that the employee does not choose to continue this agreement and said agreement shall terminate in all respects.

7. *Renegotiation*

This agreement and the attached job description may be renegotiated each year on or before the first day of April.

8. *Contractual Disputes*

This agreement shall be construed in accordance with the laws of the State of _____. If any disputes arise between the two parties to this agreement which cannot be amicably resolved between them, then any and all such disputes whether arising out of this agreement or out of the employment relationship created hereby shall be determined solely and exclusively through arbitration proceedings to be conducted pursuant to the rules of the American Arbitration Association.

The terms of this agreement are hereby accepted and executed by the undersigned on the date set forth below.

_____   _____

Employer   Date

_____   _____

Employee   Date

Appendix C

Sample Contract: Parish Life Coordinator

> In this sample contract, the arch/diocese is identified as the employer of the parish life coordinator with the parish as the paying agent. This contract includes a "for cause" provision for termination. Civil counsel should be consulted for applicable civil norms and advice before a diocese determines the form of contract to be utilized with a parish life coordinator.

Contract for Parish Life Coordinator

Arch/Diocese of _____

This contract is made this _____ day of _____, 20___, by and between the Arch/diocese of _____ (hereafter referred to a Employer) and _____ (hereafter referred to as Employee).

1. The Employer agrees to hire the above-named person as Parish Life Coordinator of _____ Parish, in (*city/town*), for the period beginning (*date*) and ending (*date*).

The Employer further agrees to provide a salary of $_____, payable by the assigned Parish, in equal installments on the _____ day(s) of each and every month, for the term of this contract (subject to the termination provisions set forth below), and subject to payroll deductions required by law and other authorized deductions. Notwithstanding that he assigned Parish will pay the salary to the Employee, it is agreed that such payments are at all times on behalf of the Arch/diocese as the sole employer, and at not time shall Employee be considered to be an employee of the assigned parish.

2. In addition to the annual salary, the Employee shall be entitled to the benefits as provided for in the attached benefit supplement of

this contract, which is incorporated herein by reference and made a part hereof. The Employee hereby accepts the terms of this contract and agrees to diligently perform the services described in the position description supplement of this contract, which is incorporated herein and made a part hereof, and to devote his or her full time and attention to the performance of his or her duties hereunder. The Employee, in the performance of the services agreed to in this contract will be accountable to the Arch/bishop of the Arch/diocese of _____ or his designee.

3. This contract is made for a three year period. If either party does not wish to renew the contract, notice in writing shall be given to the other party at least thirty (30) days before the expiration of this contract. If notice of non-renewal is not given, the contract shall automatically renew for a period of one year on the same conditions existing herein, and shall be renewed for additional one year periods if notice not to renew is not given thirty (30) days prior to expiration of any renewed contract. The Employer agrees that the Employee shall not be discharged during the term of this contract without good and sufficient cause, which shall be determined solely by the Arch/bishop of _____. In the case of such discharge, the Employer's obligations hereunder shall cease as of the date of such discharge. This contract can be terminated by the mutual agreement of both parties, in which case the responsibilities of each party shall cease. This agreement shall also be terminated by the death, or total disability, of Employee.

4. It is agreed that, solely at the option of the Arch/diocese of _ _____, the Employee may be reassigned to a difference Parish during the term of this agreement to perform the duties of Parish Life Coordinator in accordance with the attached position description. It is also agreed that the Employee may be assigned additional duties or duties different from those contained in the attached position description, so long as they are substantially related to the duties contained in the attached position description.

5. This contract is made solely between the two undersigned parties and constitutes the entire understanding with respect to the subject matter herein. There are no restrictions, promises, covenants, or undertakings other than those expressly set forth or

incorporated by reference herein. This contract supersedes all prior negotiations, agreements, and undertakings between the parties with respect to such subject matter. This agreement may only be modified in writing signed by the parties and may not be modified orally.

_____

Parish Life Coordinator (Employee)

_____

Arch/bishop of _____ (Employer)

Date: _____

Appendix D

Sample Appointment Letter

Office of the Bishop of _____

Dear (*Parish Life Coordinator*),

By means of this letter I appoint you to the office of Parish Life Coordinator of (*Parish*). Your roles and responsibilities are described in the attached position description. I also extend to you the authorizations which are listed in the enclosed document.

This appointment is effective (*Date*) and is for a term of (*Number*) years. In fulfilling your role as Parish Life Coordinator you will work with Father (*Name*) as priest supervisor. (If applicable: Father (*Name*) will provide sacramental ministry to the parish.)

Please contact my office to arrange an appropriate date for your installation ceremony in the parish. This appointment will be announced publicly in the parish on (*Date*).

(Appropriate personal and concluding remarks)

_____   _____
Bishop   Notary

(Seal)

Appendix E

Sample Installation Ceremony for Parish Life Coordinator

Ideally the diocesan bishop or his delegate should be present and preside over the installation ceremony. Other participants in and liturgical action could include the parish council chairperson, the priest supervisor, the sacramental minister if appropriate, a representative from the religious community if the parish life coordinator is a religious, and the parish life coordinator's spouse if the person is married.

Installation:

The bishop (or delegate) greets the community and offers some brief remarks on the significance of the installation ceremony. He then addresses the new Parish Life Coordinator.

BISHOP: (*Name of Parish Life Coordinator*), will you serve the people of (*Parish*) by living to the best of your ability the life of faith demanded by the Gospel and by fulfilling your role as Parish Life Coordinator?

PARISH LIFE COORDINATOR: I will.

BISHOP: Will you serve the needs of this community through the ministries of Word, Worship, Service, and Administration in accord with your responsibilities as Parish Life Coordinator?

PARISH LIFE COORDINATOR: I will.

BISHOP: Will you work with the members of this community, the priest(s) who will assist with their pastoral care, your priest supervisor, and me/your bishop, to promote a spirit of shared responsibility and respect for one another?

PARISH LIFE COORDINATOR: I will.

The bishop (or delegate) addresses the congregation:

BISHOP: Members of (*Parish*), will you received (*Parish Life Coordinator*) as your Parish Life Coordinator and give him/her the support of your prayers and your cooperation?

PEOPLE: We will.

BISHOP: (*Parish Life Coordinator*), you have expressed your willingness to serve as Parish Life Coordinator of (*Parish*).
I invite you now to receive these symbols of your ministry.

(Representative from the community come forward with a Bible, bowl of water, parish mission statement, financial records. As each gift is presented, the Parish Life Coordinator receives it and responds to the bishop as follows:)

Scripture:
BISHOP: Receive this copy of the Sacred Scriptures, the story of our salvation.

PARISH LIFE COORDINATOR: In a spirit of humility, I receive this Book of Scriptures. May I proclaim and live its message in this community so that our lives will be governed by God's holy word.

Bowl of Water.
BISHOP: Receive this sign of our common baptism in the Lord.

PARISH LIFE COORDINATOR: I joyfully receive this symbol of baptism. May I continually call forth the gifts of this baptized community in service to one another.

Parish Mission Statement.
BISHOP: Accept the mission statement of this parish community which describes their calling as followers of Christ.

PARISH LIFE COORDINATOR: I welcome this mission statement as an expression of the vision of this community and their desire to be united in heart and purpose.

Financial Records:

BISHOP: Receive the financial records of this parish in which the gifts of this community are counted and recorded.

PARISH LIFE COORDINATOR: In a spirit of stewardship I accept these records as a sign of the generosity of God's people and of my service of administration within this community.

(The Parish Life Coordinator kneels before the bishop who, with his hands extended and inviting all present to do the same, imparts his blessing.)

BISHOP: My brothers and sisters, pray with me that God will give his blessings to (*Parish life coordinator*) who has been chosen for ministry within this community.

Loving God, Source of all we have and are, we praise you.

Give your blessing to (*Parish Life Coordinator*) that he/she may be an instrument of your care for the people of this parish.

By his/her life and faith may he/she show forth your Word of Truth and celebrate your presence in love and joy.

Through prayer and good works may he/she grow in knowledge of you.

May he/she call forth the gifts of this community, allowing others to offer their services and to minister as they have been called to do.

We make our prayer through Jesus Christ you Son, our Lord, who lives and reigns with you and the Holy Spirit, one God, forever and ever.

ALL: Amen.

Sample Mandate from the Presybteral Moderator to the Parish Life Coordinator[120]

SAINT PROCOP CATHOLIC CHURCH
Cleveland, Ohio

I, (Name), Presbyteral Moderator of the Church of Saint Procop, Cleveland, Ohio, assigned by the Bishop of Cleveland (date) for a term of three years, grant (Name), Parish Life Coordinator of the Church of Saint Procop, Cleveland, Ohio, assigned by the Bishop of Cleveland (date) for a term of three years, the following responsibilities to be carried out according to the norms of canon law and civil law.

These mandates are to be in effect for as long as the Parish Life Coordinator holds office unless they are amended or revoked after consultation with the Bishop of Cleveland or his delegate.

- Canonical representation of the parish: You are to be the canonical representative of Saint Procop Parish in accord with the laws of the Church, both universal law and particular law;

- Civil legal representation: You are to be the civil legal representative of Saint Procop Parish in accord with the laws of the appropriate civil jurisdiction;

- Parish Council representation: You are to preside at meetings of the parish council;

- Finance Council representation: You are to preside at meetings of the parish finance council;

- Administrative decisions: You are to make all decisions

---

[120] The model for the above mandate may be found in *Empowerment for Ministry: A Complete Manual on Diocesan Faculties for Priests, Deacons, and Lay Ministers* by John M. Huels, J.C.D., (New York/Mahwah: Paulist Press, 2003) 248.

necessary for the duties in your job description and for enacting pastoral plans and parish projects;

• Decisions restricting the right to the sacraments: Decisions which restrict the right to the sacramental life of the Church require the consultation and consent of the presbyteral moderator. In his absence, you may decide the matter after consultation with the chancellor of the Diocese of Cleveland.

_____

Signature of Presbyteral Moderator

I accept the mandates given above by the Presbyteral Moderator.

_____

Signature of Parish Life Coordinator

_____

Date

Parish Seal

SELECTED BIBLIOGRAPHY

Books

Beal, John P. Et al. *New Commentary of the Code of Canon Law*. New York/Mahwah, NJ: Paulist Press, 2000.

Beeman, Dennis, et. al. *Pastoral Coordinators: Parish Leadership without a Resident Pastor*. New York: National Pastoral Life Center, 1995.

Burkart, Gary. *The Parish Life Coordinator*. Kansas City, MO: Sheed and Ward, 1992.

Chandler, Mary Moisson. *The Pastoral Associate and the Lay Pastor*. Collegeville, MN: The Liturgical Press, 1986.

Code of Canon Law Latin-English Edition New English Translation (Washington: CLSA, 1999).

Cusack, Barbara Anne, and Therese Guerin Sullivan, SP. *Pastoral Care in Parishes without a Pastor: Applications of Canon 517, §2*. Washington: CLSA, 1995.

Euart, Sharon, RSM. *Pastoral Coordinators and Canon Law*. New York: National Pastoral Life Center, 1995.

Huels, John M. *Empowerment for Ministry: A Complete Manual on Diocesan Faculties for Priests, Deacons, and Lay Ministers*. New York/Mahwah, NJ: Paulist Press, 2003.

------------. *The Pastoral Companion: A Canon Law Handbook for Catholic Ministry*. Quincy, IL: Franciscan Press, 2002.

Klister, Roy. *Non-Presbyteral Pastoral Care in Parish Liturgical Life*. Wrightstown, WI: R.M. Klister, 1991.

Monette, Maurice, O.M.I. *Partners in Ministry: Priests in Collaboration with Parish Life Coordinators.* Kansas City, MO: Sheed and
Ward, 1988.

Murnion, Philip, et. al. *New Parish. Ministers.* New York: National
Pastoral Life Center, 1992.

Vadakumthala, Alexander. *Lay Person as Caretakers of a Parish.*
Rome: Pontifical Urban University, 1992.

ARTICLES

Bittner, Gregory T. "Tensions in Achieving and Observing Subsidiarity," *CLSA Proceedings* 65 (2003) 1-30.

Budney, Linda. "The Parish as Employer," *CLSA Proceedings* 64
(2002) 59-72.

Congregation of the Clergy, *The Priest, Pastor and Leader of the
Parish Community,* August 4, 2002 in *L'Osservatore Romano,*
English Edition, January 14, 2003.

*Ecclesiae de mysterio, On Certain Questions Regarding the
Collaboration of the Non-Ordained Faithful in the Sacred Ministry
of Priests.* 15 August 1997 in *AAS* 89 (1997) 852-877.

Foster, John J.M. "The Relationship of Public and Private Worship,"
CLSA Proceedings 64 (2002) 121-143.

Huels, John M. "Ministry to the Sick and Dying in View of the
Shortage of Priests," *CLSA Proceedings* 63 (2001) 127-146.

-----------. "Principles of Liturgical Adaptation in Light of Justice and
Forgiveness," *CLSA Proceedings* 61 (1999) 1-25.

----------. "Preparation for the Sacraments: Faith, Rights," *Studia
Canonica* 28 (1994) 33-58.

McDonough, Kevin M. "Beyond Bureaucracy: New Strategies for Diocesan Leadership," *CLSA Proceedings* 61 (1999) 251-265.

Pagé, Roch. "The Principle of Subsidiarity Revisited," *CLSA Proceedings* 64 (2002) 191-208.

Palmieri, Alexander J. "Parishes Entrusted to the Card of Religious: Starting Afresh from Christ," *CLSA Proceedings* 64 (2002) 209-239.

Ramírez, Ricardo, CSB, and Catherine Darcy, RSM. "Canonical Ministry to Migrants," *CLSA Proceedings* 63 (2001) 215-232.

Rehrauer, Ann, OSF. "Current Issues in Liturgical and Sacramental Law," *CLSA Proceedings* 62 (2000) 245-262.

Renken, John A. "The Parish: Community of the Christian Faithful within the Particular Church," *CLSA Proceedings* 60 (1998) 179-223.

Rinere, Elissa A. CP. "Canonical Education of Official Church Ministers," *CLSA Proceedings* 57 (1995) 325-336.

Wijlens, Myriam. "Ecclesial Lay Ministry, Clergy and Complementarity," *CLSA Proceedings* 64 (2002) 27-47.

CONTRIBUTORS

Sister Therese Guerin Sullivan is a member of the Sisters of Providence who earned a Masters in Education from De Paul University in 1975; a doctorate in ministry from St. Mary of the Lake, Mundelein in 1987 and a JCL degree from St. Paul University, Ottawa, Canada, in 1989.

Reverend Gary D. Yanus is a presbyter of the Diocese of Cleveland, Ohio, and a member of the CLSA since 1984. He earned a Master of Divinity from St. Mary Seminary in Cleveland in 1981 and a JCD degree from St. Thomas in Urbe, Rome, Italy in 1986. Both canonists live and minister in the Diocese of Cleveland, Ohio.

THE CANON LAW SOCIETY OF AMERICA

Membership in the Canon Law Society of America is open to interested persons who wish to collaborate in the promotion of the pastoral ministry of the Church within the context of its legal/canonical structures. Membership of non-Catholic persons is also welcomed.

The Society's constitution identifies four (4) kinds of membership: Active, Associate, Student, and Honorary. Active membership is open to those who have earned at least a licentiate degree in canon law; active membership is also open to other practitioners in canon law who demonstrate a broadly based competence in canonical issues and who have fulfilled the stipulated requirements established by the Board of Governors of the Society as enumerated in the By-Laws. Associate members are any others who wish to associate themselves with the purpose of the Society. Student membership is open to those enrolled in any school of canon law engaged in studies to obtain a licentiate degree in canon law. Student members enjoy the same prerogatives as associate members in the Society. Honorary members are (a) *ex officio* all the Most Reverend Bishops of the United States, and (b) those persons, who by reason of outstanding contributions in the filed of canon law or in support of the Society, are proposed for this distinction of honorary membership by the Board of Governors and accepted by a majority vote of the active members at the General Meeting.

Membership information and applications are available from the Office of the Executive Coordinator. An application may also be downloaded from the web at www.clsa.org. Payment of the initial dues is required with the submission of the application.

For questions and further information, please contact:

Office of the Executive Coordinator
Canon Law Society of America
108 North Payne Street, Suite C
Alexandria, VA 22314-2906
Tel: 703/739-2560
Fax: 703/739-2562
E-mail: coordinator@clsa.org.